FULFILLMENT

Fulfillment

Joyce Marie Smith

TYNDALE HOUSE PUBLISHERS, INC.
Wheaton, Illinois

To Ted
who has encouraged
and helped me find
fulfillment as a
person, wife, and
mother,

Thirteenth printing, June 1984

Library of Congress Catalog Card Number 75-15194
ISBN 8423-0980-2
Copyright © 1975 by Tyndale House Publishers, Inc.,
Wheaton, Illinois
Printed in the United States of America

Contents

The Woman Fulfilled As a Mother
Her Spiritual Responsibilities and Blessings

Preface

It's exciting to be a woman! At no time in history has a woman had as much freedom or as many opportunities as today.

Yet many women are frustrated and unhappy and *unfulfilled*.

This Bible Study is designed to help you to be glad you are a woman, and to enable you in finding total fulfillment as an individual in your relationship with God, as a wife and mother, or as a single woman.

Whatever your status or position or situation is in life, you can find *total fulfillment,* purpose, and joy.

This study can be used in two ways:

1. The Bible Study group can come together, look up the Scripture and answer the questions together in the group.

2. The students can prepare and answer the questions ahead of time, and then share their answers in the discussion group.

Joyce Marie Smith

Suggestions for the Leader

1. If the group is larger than 12-15 you might consider breaking up into several smaller groups (such as a large Sunday school class).

2. If you have less than one hour for your study, you could eliminate some of the questions, or perhaps divide into several groups with each group assigned a portion of the study. After a designated period, you could all come back together and summarize the high points of each group.

Self-Preparation

1. Complete the lesson each week. If you have time, read some of the references for background material.

2. Before you lead, ask the Lord to cleanse you of any known sin, and ask to be filled with the Holy Spirit. We need to be controlled by the Holy Spirit as we guide the discussion.

3. Pray for sensitivity to the needs of the women in your group.

4. Ask God to give you enthusiasm, and to make you an interesting leader.

5. Ask for love and humility as you lead.

6. Pray for authority from God.

Guiding the Discussion

1. Don't allow tangents to develop. Bring the discussion back to the topic.

2. Discourage discussion on controversial issues.

3. Don't get bogged down with a question that doesn't stimulate interest or discussion—go on to the next question.

4. Be concerned for the quiet one who never speaks up. Call on her if you can see she has done her lesson, or ask her opinion.

5. If someone gives a definitely wrong answer, ask for another opinion.

6. If you can't answer a question, say, "Why don't we do some research on that question this week?"

7. Do not take advantage of your position as leader to talk excessively and give all the answers or comment on every question.

Additional Ideas

1. For a large group, you may want to vary the format occasionally by having a panel discussion (you could use the questions from the study); a guest speaker on a particular subject; have book reports from some of the suggested books; etc.

The Woman Fulfilled As a Person

Her Self-Image
LESSON 1: Do You Like Yourself?

A woman can't accept and love her parents, boss, friends, or husband as they are until she first accepts and loves herself as God made her. Our own self-image is directly related to our understanding of God's completed work for our lives. Our self-image is a composite of all our past relationships and experiences, and has a definite effect on our personality and emotions.

1. Fill in the chart below describing how I feel about myself.

	How I feel	*How I wish I felt*
Parents		
Childhood		
Economic Background		
Appearance		
Abilities		
Relationship to God		

2. List my *strengths* and *weaknesses*
   How has God helped me overcome my weaknesses?

3. List situations where I feel threatened. How do I react?

4. When and where do I feel more sure of myself?

Two excellent new books on self-image and self-acceptance are James Dobson's book *Hide or Seek*[1], and *Do I Have to Be Me?*[2] by Lloyd Ahlem.

How Does God Feel About Me?

5. How does God look at me? Summarize briefly these verses.

    a. Romans 3:21-26
    b. Psalm 139:1-3, 13-16
    c. Isaiah 45:9-11
    d. John 3:16
    e. Isaiah 43:7
    f. Ephesians 2:10
    g. Ephesians 2:22
    h. Philippians 1:6

Things to think about:

    a. What am I telling God if I don't like myself?
    b. How does my self-image affect my relationship with other people?
    c. How can I compare myself to anyone else if I am uniquely made—if there is no one else exactly like me? If I continually compare myself with others, it encourages either an inferiority complex or a superiority complex to develop.
    d. Do I engage in self-criticism (putting myself

[1] James Dobson, *Hide or Seek* (New Jersey: Fleming Revell, 1974).
[2] Lloyd Ahlem, *Do I Have to Be Me?* (Glendale: Regal, 1973).

down) hoping others will disagree and build up my ego?

How Can I Increase My Self-Love?

Joyce Landorf stresses the importance of completely accepting God's forgiveness in her chapter, "The Poised Beauty of Self-Acceptance."[3]

6. In order to experience total forgiveness and self-love I need to realize the importance of these principles:
   a. Accept God's forgiveness (Ephesians 1:4, *The Living Bible;* 1 John 1:7-9). As I confess my sins, he has promised to _____.
   b. In Matthew 22:37-39 I am commanded to love
      _____, _____, _____.
   c. As I accept God's love, I can ask him to teach me how to love myself.

7. How can I help a friend, husband, or child who has a low self-image?

My Application:

If I need to improve my self-image and self-acceptance:

a. Thank God that he loves me and ask him to help me love myself.
b. Accept his forgiveness.
c. Realize God has a special plan just for me.
d. Thank God for what he is going to do in me.

[3]Joyce Landorf, *The Fragrance of Beauty* (Wheaton: Victor Books, 1973) pp. 90-105.

Her Emotions
LESSON 2: Are You Up or Down?

Every human being experiences a change of moods, and these can be caused by success or failure, circumstances, physical health or conditions, and even the weather (such as a depressing fog), but there are also moods which are directly related to the woman's monthly cycle. It is important that a woman understand herself and the changes that take place during this period. However, we must remember not to depend on our emotions or feelings, but on God's Word and faithfulness. He can help us become more stable and steady in our disposition.

Emotions and Moods

1. What are emotions and moods?

2. What is personality?

One helpful tool in understanding my own personality is to recognize the four basic temperaments which Dr. Tim LaHaye discusses.[1] As I understand the strengths and weaknesses of my basic temperament, I can better

[1]Tim LaHaye, *Spirit-Controlled Temperament* (Wheaton: Tyndale, 1966) Ch. 3-5.

accept myself. As I bring God my weaknesses, I can experience his working in my life.

3. What emotions were shown in these women's lives:
   a. Eve—Genesis 3:7-10
   b. Hannah—1 Samuel 1:5, 7, 10
   c. Mary Magdalene—Luke 7:37, 38
   d. Women at the cross—Luke 23:27
   e. Woman with hemorrhage—Mark 5:27-33
   What are some other emotions I experience?

4. Describe the feelings I have which tend to get me down. What are the causes?

Depression

Depression is a common problem among women. It can be caused by circumstances, physical, mental, or spiritual sources. According to Dr. Tim LaHaye, *anger* and *self-pity* easily result in depression.

5. List the emotions in these verses which also can cause depression.
   a. Matthew 6:25-34
   b. Ecclesiastes 7:9
   c. 2 Timothy 1:7
   d. Psalms 40:12

Also, people who become easily depressed usually have a problem with their self-image, since they don't think very highly of themselves.[2]

6. Dr. Tim LaHaye's suggestions[3] as how to overcome depression are:

[2]Tim LaHaye, *How to Win over Depression* (Grand Rapids: Zondervan, 1974) pp. 137-159.
[3]From *Spirit-Controlled Temperament* by Tim LaHaye (Wheaton, Illinois: Tyndale House Publishers) pp. 115-117.

a. Confess your anger or self-pity as sin.

b. Ask God to take away the habit pattern, and give you victory.

c. Have a thankful attitude.

d. Ask to be filled with the Holy Spirit.

7. What helps in overcoming depression are found in these verses?

a. Isaiah 61:3

b. 1 John 1:9

c. 1 Thessalonians 5:18

d. Romans 8:28-39

My Application

1. What one emotion or personality trait do I especially want Christ to control?

2. What specific area will I ask Christ to work on in my life this week?

A helpful book on this subject is *A Gracious Woman* by Mrs. W. David Stuart, published by the Warr Foundation.

Her Physical Appearance — Femininity
LESSON 3: It's Fun to Be a Woman

Since femininity accentuates the differences between men and women, it stands to reason that a feminine woman makes a man feel more masculine. It also arouses responsibility in him—he will want to take care of you. Femininity begins with an attitude—an acceptance of yourself as a woman. If you don't accept and fulfill this role in life, the result will be frustration, rebellion and confusion and unhappiness. If a woman tries to become like a man in looks or aggressiveness, or compete with him, she is cheating herself of her beautiful femininity. It really is fun to be a woman!

Read 1 Corinthians 6:19, 20. This is our criterion—that our bodies belong to God, and our physical appearance is important because it affects our witness as Christian women.

What Is the Importance of Looking, Feeling and Being Feminine?

1. What is the definition of *femininity?*

2. Femininity affects the way I feel about myself, the way I relate to men, the way I act. Discuss why I agree or disagree with this statement.

3. What does 1 Samuel 16:7 say about the outward appearance?
4. How does my self-image affect my outward appearance?

Effect of Diet

5. What are some basic foods which should be included in a well-balanced diet?
6. a. What are some foods which harm the complexion, health, or figure?
   b. What is the effect of diet on the personality?
7. Do I make an effort to eat properly? If not, why? If I am overweight, what specifically am I doing to correct this problem?

Some excellent resource books on nutrition are *Let's Eat Right to Keep Fit*[1] and *Secrets of Health and Beauty*[2]. There are organizations such as Weight Watchers and TOPS that encourage proper diets (and recipes!) and exercising.

How Can I Become More Feminine?

There are certain colors (pastels, florals, polka dots), materials (soft, fluid), and basic cuts (not too tailored) which are traditionally feminine.

8. Do you feel you dress in a feminine or masculine way? Why?

One principle a Christian woman should apply to her dress is that it should never hinder or detract from her verbal witness. Be feminine for God himself. Dress as his child.

[1]Adelle Davis, *Let's Eat Right to Keep Fit* (New York: Harcourt, Brace & Worold, 1954).
[2]Linda Clark, *Secrets of Health and Beauty* (New York: Pyramid, 1969).

Inner Beauty

To give forth the sweet fragrance of Christ (2 Corinthians 2:14, 15) involves not only our outward appearance but an inner beauty of our soul. Inner beauty is not characterized by fear, anxiety, worry, anger, or hate. These emotions must be brought under the influence and control of the Holy Spirit. *Fragrance of Beauty* is a lovely book describing how one can have this outer and inner beauty.[3]

9. Summarize what these verses say about inner beauty.
   a. 1 Peter 3:3, 4
   b. Proverbs 31:30
   c. 2 Corinthians 2:14, 15
   d. Galatians 5:22, 23

   Qualities of a gentle and quiet spirit are to be:
   1. spiritually minded
   2. submissive—1 Peter 3:3, 4
   3. obedient to Lord
   4. unfearful—2 Timothy 1:8

I may not be able to do much about my basic physical appearance, but I can have a Spirit-controlled personality and develop inner beauty.

My Application

1. What specific things am I going to do this week to be more feminine and develop inner beauty? (reading appropriate books, etc.)

2. Remember: a woman's appearance, her weight, and inner beauty indicate who is in control of her life.

[3]Joyce Landorf, *The Fragrance of Beauty* (Wheaton: Victor, 1973).

The Woman Fulfilled Spiritually

Her Relationship to Christ
LESSON 4: Do You Belong to the Family of God?

Fulfillment is found not in one's circumstances but in the attitudes of the heart. It is important that our study on the woman—her problems, purpose, and potentials—be based on the premise that our ultimate individual fulfillment can be found only in Jesus Christ. What a privilege to have a personal relationship with the God of the universe! He made you and longs to fellowship with you. To see the depths of his personal interest in *you,* read Psalm 139.

My Need

1. First, I must realize why I need Christ. Summarize briefly these verses.

   a. Romans 3:23

   b. Romans 5:12

   c. Romans 6:23

   d. Jeremiah 17:9

2. If I am separated from God by my sin, how can I have a relationship with him?

   a. Romans 5:8; Christ _____ for me.

   b. John 14:6; Christ claimed to be the _____,

the _____, and the _____, the only way to God. As my friend Ken Poure says, "Some claim this is too narrow. . . . did you ever stop to think that every person on this planet got here *one way?!*"

Claims of Christ:

1. John 4:14—Giver of everlasting water
2. John 5:17, 18—Equality with God (Also John 10:30)
3. John 5:24—Giver of eternal life
4. John 5:37, 43—Sent of God
5. John 6:35, 48, 51—Bread of life
6. John 8:12—Light of the world
7. John 8:58—I AM
8. John 10:11—Good Shepherd
9. John 10:7, 9—Door
10. John 11:25—Resurrection and Life
11. John 14:6—Way, Truth, and Life

My Action

3. In order to receive eternal life and have this relationship with God, what must I do?
   a. What is the key word in John 3:16 _____;
      John 1:12 _____, _____.
   b. Revelation 3:20 shows me I must take what action?
4. 1 John 5:11, 12 and John 5:24 tells what God guarantees to those who have his Son. _____

My Assurance

5. What assurance can I have that I have eternal life? Give a phrase from these verses:

    a. 1 John 5:11-13

    b. Hebrews 7:24, 25

6. Have I asked Jesus Christ to be my own personal Savior?   If not, why?

7. List below the results of asking Christ to be Savior.

    a. 1 John 1:9; Colossians 1:14

    b. John 1:12

    c. 2 Corinthians 5:17

    d. Galatians 5:22, 23

    e. John 10:10

    f. Philippians 4:13

    g. John 16:24

    h. 1 John 4:4

Are there any other results that I have experienced?

My Application

1. Write out a prayer letter to Jesus Christ of love or commitment.

Freedom from Hangups
LESSON 5: Are You an Overcomer?

Many believers are on a guilt trip—dwelling on their past failures or past sins. The results of guilt range from condemnation to depression and even suicide. God desires that we live victorious, liberated lives.

God's Forgiveness
1. How can I become free from guilt? By totally recognizing and accepting the extent of God's complete forgiveness. Summarize these verses.
   a. Psalm 103:12
   b. Micah 7:19
   c. Isaiah 44:22
   d. Jeremiah 31:34
   e. Hebrews 9:22
   f. 1 John 1:7, 9

God's forgiveness is total and complete. My acceptance in God's eyes is not based on my performance or actions, but my position in Christ.

Freedom from Guilt
Hal Lindsey has written an excellent booklet which discusses the causes and effects of guilt.[1]

[1]Hal Lindsey, *The Guilt Trip* (Grand Rapids: Zondervan, 1972).

2. How to experience freedom from guilt:
   a. Confess my sins (1 John 1:7-9)
   b. Accept God's Sacrifice (Hebrews 9:12; 1 Peter 1:18, 19)
   c. Claim cleansing of my mind (Hebrews 9:13, 14; 10:10, 22)
   d. Claim victory from condemnation (Romans 8:1, 2)
   e. If necessary, become reconciled with your brother (Matthew 5:23, 24)

Perhaps my hang-up isn't guilt but fear . . . or anxiety . . . or resentment . . . or self-pity . . . or selfishness . . . or depression . . . or anger . . . or an unforgiving or critical spirit. . . . Christ wants to liberate me from these carnal characteristics—Luke 4:18.

My Enemy

As a Christian, I need also to recognize who my enemy is and how he attacks me.

3. How is Satan described in these verses:
   a. 1 Peter 5:8
   b. Ephesians 6:12
   c. 2 Corinthians 11:14

4. How am I told to deal with Satan in these verses?
   a. James 4:7
   b. 1 Peter 5:8, 9
   c. Revelation 12:11
   d. Ephesians 6:10-18

5. How does Satan attack me? Share a recent experience of an attack of Satan that you have had.

24

An excellent resource book on the nature and work of Satan is *Satan Is Alive and Well on Planet Earth*.[2]

The Spirit-Filled Walk

All Christians are indwelt by the Holy Spirit but not all Christians are controlled and filled with the Holy Spirit.

6. What command is given in Ephesians 5:18?
7. What are some functions of the Holy Spirit?
   a. John 14:16
   b. John 14:17
   c. John 14:26
   d. John 15:26
   e. John 16:8
   f. John 16:13
8. How can I appropriate the power of the Holy Spirit?
   a. Luke 11:11-13
   b. John 7:37-39
9. The results of the Spirit-controlled life are exciting!
   a. Galatians 5:22, 23
   b. Acts 1:8
   c. Ephesians 3:16-20
   We need to be plugged in to our source of POWER!

My Application:

1. Take one of the hang-ups listed that is a problem and find as many Scriptures as you can that relate to it. Claim God's Word for this problem area.
2. Bring any sins and wrong attitudes to God, asking his forgiveness and cleansing, and claim his deliverance in your life. Ask his filling of the Holy Spirit.

[2]Hal Lindsey, *Satan Is Alive and Well on Planet Earth* (Grand Rapids: Zondervan, 1972).

Her Purpose and Responsibilities
LESSON 6: What Are You Here For?

As she abides in Christ, a woman can have total fulfillment and satisfaction in her present calling. God has a wonderful purpose and plan for each woman, whether she is single or married.

God's Purpose for Me

1. God has a purpose for my life. What is his general purpose for all believers from these verses: Romans 8:29; Revelation 4:11; Ephesians 4:13; and 1 Corinthians 1:9.

    a.

    b.

    c.

    d.

2. God has a special purpose for women. What is it? Genesis 1:28; 2:18; and 1 Corinthians 11:9.

3. If the commandment in Genesis 1:28 was given to both man and woman, how can a woman fulfill this command?

    a. Be fruitful and multiply. (How am I now reproducing myself?)

    b. Replenish the earth. (How am I now replenishing the earth?)

c. Subdue the earth. (How am I now subduing the earth?)

What additional things could I be doing to fulfill this command?

Women God Has Used

4. God has used women throughout history to fulfill his purpose. Pick three of the following women and note how God used them.
   a. Sarah—Genesis 12:1, 2; Genesis 17:15, 16
   b. Rahab—Joshua 6:23, 24; Matthew 1:5; Hebrews 11:31
   c. Ruth—Ruth 1:16; 4:13-17; Matthew 1:5
   d. Esther—Esther 4:14
   e. Mary—Matthew 1:21
   f. Anna—Luke 2:36-38

5. List the activities these women were involved in:
   a. Phoebe—Romans 16:1, 2
   b. Priscilla—Acts 18:2, 3, 24-26; Romans 16:3, 4
   c. Miriam—Exodus 15:20
   d. Deborah—Judges 4:4
   e. Esther—Esther 7:3, 4
   f. Lydia—Acts 16:14

6. Proverbs 31 describes the activities and characteristics of the virtuous woman. List them.

7. List the responsibilities I have right now. Am I fulfilling them?

My Application:

1. What specific purpose in life do I have right now?

2. What specific things could I be doing right now to fulfill this?

Her Ministry
LESSON 7: Are You Using Your Gifts?

A ministry basically means to help, serve or comfort someone—to care about people. It involves a giving of ourselves. There are many types of ministry, and it helps if you know what your spiritual gifts are. Rick Yohn has written an excellent book on this subject.[1]

1. After reading Romans 12:3-8; 1 Corinthians 12:27-31; and Ephesians 4:11-13, I will pray and ask God to show me my spiritual gift(s). List below the gift(s) I feel I have.

2. What kind of ministry do I have now? How much time do I spend each week helping someone else?

3. What are some types of ministry I would like to have?

4. Think of someone who has needs. List her needs. Pray for her.

Witnessing

Our most important ministry with non-Christian friends is sharing our faith with them. Some people have the gift of evangelism (Ephesians 4:11-13) but every-

---

[1]Rick Yohn, *Discover Your Spiritual Gift and Use It* (Wheaton: Tyndale, 1974) pp. 1-7.

one is commanded to witness (Acts 1:8; Luke 24:48). There are many valuable tools to help in witnessing, such as the "Four Spiritual Laws" by Campus Crusade.[2]

5. What are some approaches and verses I have found valuable in my witnessing?

6. What problems or difficulties have I experienced in my witnessing?

7. Do I need more training or help to be a better witness?

8. Who was the last person I witnessed to and when?

Creativity

We are created in God's image. He is the Creator of all things, so we can be and are made to be creative also. As Christian women we should have a real freedom in developing creativity that touches all areas of our lives. Creativity does involve some risk because it expresses our inner self.

In *Hidden Art,* Edith Schaeffer suggests many ways to be creative from flower arranging to music, from interior decorating to drama. For instance, in her chapter on Food she suggests many ways to vary basic foods so you don't get into a rut—how to be imaginative, and yet economical.[3]

9. Things to Do: List some creative projects you would like to do, such as making decoupage, ceramics, decorating a room, entertaining, etc.

   1.
   2.

[2]*The Four Spiritual Laws* (Campus Crusade for Christ, 1965).
[3]Edith Schaeffer, *Hidden Art* (Wheaton: Tyndale, 1971).

3.

4.

What values are there in trying to become more creative?

Hospitality

Hospitality can bring great joy to the guest as well as the host.[4] This virtue has always been esteemed by civilized people. Single women can have a special ministry in entertaining.

10. Who was entertained in Genesis 18:2, 3; Hebrews 13:2? ˆ

11. What is commanded in Romans 12:3, and 1 Peter 4:9?

12. What was a prerequisite of a bishop or pastor in 1 Timothy 3:2 and Titus 1:8?

13. What are some characteristics of a gracious hostess?

Application

1. Have I found out what my spiritual gifts are and am I using them?

2. What ministry do I have in my church?

3. What am I doing to become a better witness?

4. What areas do I need to improve in to become a better hostess?

[4]Gladys Hunt, *MS Means Myself* (Grand Rapids: Zondervan, 1972).

The Single Woman Fulfilled

Her Completeness, and Problems to Cope With

LESSON 8: How to Be Alone but Not Lonely

Look at the statistics—109 women to every 100 men. It is difficult for a girl to be prepared for marriage or to remain single. Some girls are so resigned to being single they have no hope or expectancy and others will do anything to get married, whether the man is God's choice for them or not. Let's remember our first purpose is to glorify God, to enjoy him, and to please him. Rather than looking for the right man, you can be becoming the right woman. Marriage is a gift and a specific calling from God. He has a wonderful timing in each of our lives and a beautiful plan. The single years can be a real time of growth . . . yes, you can be alone and like it!

Well, at this point, you are single. What are some of the problems you face? Our premise is that God understands all your needs and wants to meet them. 1 Peter 5:7

Loneliness

There is nothing unusual about being lonely—it is universal. One can be lonely in the midst of a crowd. Let's face our loneliness and do something about it. Have definite goals, schedules, and plans. Special times of loneliness can be evenings, holidays, and times of illness. Gini Andrews has some good suggestions on handling loneliness in *Your Half of the Apple*.[1]

1. List 5 specific ways to keep from becoming lonely.
   a.
   b.
   c.
   d.
   e.

2. Do you think Christ experienced loneliness?
   What are some promises of God to me?
   a. Matthew 28:20
   b. Hebrews 13:5

Love

Love is a basic human need. *MS Means Myself*[2] discusses this need.

3. What needs will God supply? Philippians 4:19

4. How can my own need for love be met?
   Look at these promises of love: John 3:16; 15:9; 12-14; 1 John 4:7-12.

SINGLE PEOPLE are especially vulnerable to certain problems or sins such as:

   a. Self-pity (poor me! I don't even have a boyfriend!)
   b. Anger (bitterness or resentment over being single or homely or fat or . . .)

[1]Gini Andrews, *Your Half of the Apple* (Grand Rapids: Zondervan, 1972), ch. 12.
[2]Gladys Hunt, *MS Means Myself* (Grand Rapids, Zondervan, 1972), pp. 111, 112.

    c. Jealousy (of married or engaged couples; over-sensitive to people's remarks)
    d. Selfishness (you have no one else to think about but yourself)
    e. Insecurity (remember, our only real security is in God himself)

The Unmarried Woman[3] also elaborates on the problems and solutions for the single girl. Now let's look at some of the advantages.

Advantages

    a. Being called to and involved in a large purpose for God
    b. Spending more time alone with God
    c. A ministry of Christian service which would be difficult with a mate (1 Corinthians 7:8, 26, 28, 29, 32, 34, 35)
    d. Freedom to make unlimited friendships
    e. Freedom to discover and develop new talents and abilities
    f. Living and traveling abroad
    g. Finances—usually not supporting anyone else.

Can you think of other advantages?

Male Companionship

In 1 Corinthians 11:11, 12 we find a dependent relationship between male and female. Ephesians 5:21 commands a mutual submissiveness. A woman needs male companionship and contacts to enhance her femininity and to enlarge and complement her perspective on life. In

[3]Clyde Narramore, *The Unmarried Woman* (Grand Rapids: Zondervan, 1961).

order to meet men, you must get out of your apartment and be in the mainstream of life. Possibilities are unlimited: 1. Church and all its activities; 2. retreats and conferences; 3. sports (swimming, golf, skiing, tennis, cycling, bowling); 4. classes (school or other); 5. mutual friends; 6. your work.

My Application

Remember, "The joy of the Lord is your strength" Nehemiah 8:10.

1. What specific actions will help me to achieve personal fulfillment?

2. In what specific areas did the lesson convict me?

3. What changes do I need in my attitudes?

Her Relationships with Others
LESSON 9: Friendly Relations

One of God's gifts to us is the beautiful, deep relationship we can have with other people. We need close friends that we can be completely open and honest with, sharing our innermost feelings and ambitions. A friend is one who accepts us as we are—who has learned to keep a confidence, and is one we can trust.

1. What are characteristics of true fellowship? 1 John 1:3; Colossians 3:16; and 1 Corinthians 12.

2. What kind of friend do we need? Proverbs 17:17; 18:24.

Parental Relations

3. How do I feel towards my parents?

4. What command is given in Ephesians 6:1; Exodus 20:12?

   a. How can I demonstrate my faith at home?

   b. Am I willing to change my plans to please my parents?

   c. In what specific ways can I be more considerate and honoring of my parents?

Female Friendships

5. a. What kind of a friend should I be? Proverbs
   17:17; 27:9, 10
   b. What are some characteristics I like in a friend?

6. How do I give of myself to others?

7. What can ruin a friendship? Proverbs 16:28; 17:9;
   25:17
   Do I compete or feel threatened by other girls?
   Am I jealous or envious of my friends?

8. How does John 13:35 apply?
   Is there any friend right now that I have a problem
   with? I need not only to confess this sin to God, but
   also to the friend. (See Matthew 5:22-24; 6:15; Mark
   11:25; James 5:16.)

Male Friendships

We need to not be in pursuit of marriage in order to
have healthy male friendships. Rather than always asking,
"Is this the one?" you can learn to be friends, to minister
to each other, to build each other up in the Lord. It is
very important to accept your male friend.

Male friendships are good preparation for friendship
in marriage. Friendships help develop many areas of
your life and personality. Men can broaden your understanding of humanity and give a male perspective to
your life. Don't let premature pressure towards marriage
spoil your relationship. Audrey Sands's book, *Single and
Satisfied*[1] discusses these areas.

9. What does Ecclesiastes 3:7b say on timing of
   friendships?

[1] Audrey Sands, *Single and Satisfied* (Wheaton: Tyndale, 1971).

10. It is important not to let my mind fantasize my relationship. How can I help a man so he doesn't feel trapped or chased?

11. What are things I look for in a man?

12. What are some important reasons for "mutual submission" as commanded in Ephesians 5:22?

13. How are Christian men to treat younger women? 1 Timothy 5:1, 2

14. What should be some characteristics of my relationship? Colossians 3:12-17; 1 Peter 5:5; Galatians 5:13-15, 6:2

My Application

1. What areas of my friendships do I need to reevaluate and change?

2. How can I be a better friend to others?

3. Do I need to improve my relationship with my parents?

Her Dating Standards and Morality
LESSON 10: Should You Say No?

As we focus on the area of dating, let's begin by evaluating our attitudes. Dating can be a great learning experience. The standards we have are very important because they affect future relationships with men, potential happiness in marriage and our self-image.

Diversified Dating:

The purposes of diversified dating are:

a. It brings appreciation of the differences in masculine and feminine viewpoints.

b. It helps us understand differences in personality and temperament.

c. It helps keep a check on the emotions.

d. It builds self-confidence with the opposite sex.

1. Write down several characteristics I look for in a prospective date. Remember, you will end up marrying someone you once dated . . . therefore you should not seriously date a person that you would not want to marry.

God's Will for You—Morality

It is because of God's love and concern that he forbids premarital sex. God wants to protect you. Yes, you should say no to premarital sex!

2. Summarize each of the following verses concerning immorality.

    a. 1 Corinthians 6:9, 13, 18-20
    b. 1 Thessalonians 4:3-5
    c. Hebrews 13:4
    d. Galatians 5:19
    e. Colossians 3:5
    f. 1 Peter 1:16
    g. Matthew 15:18, 19

Sexual Understanding before Marriage[1] is an excellent book which discusses all aspects of sex, as well as reasons for premarital chastity.

Sex is a powerful drive—it's the desire to enter into a total union with another personality. The reasons for chastity are to protect you physically, emotionally, spiritually, and mentally as well as to protect your future marriage.

3. Listed below are some reasons for chastity.

Physical Protection

Premarital pregnancy (or abortion)
Venereal disease
See 1 Corinthians 6:18-20

Spiritual Protection

As sin it breaks fellowship with God

---

[1]Herbert Miles, *Sexual Understanding before Marriage* (Grand Rapids: Zondervan, 1971).

(1 Corinthians 6:9, 10; also 6:15-20
It hardens your heart towards God

Emotional and Mental Protection

Causes guilt, insecurity
Disintegrates your personality
Causes lack of trust of each other (even after marriage)
Makes you feel trapped (often results in an unhappy
   marriage)
Damages your self-respect and self-image
Read Psalm 32:3, 4; Psalm 51
Also affects your feelings towards men (such as
   "They are using me.")

Premarital sex is a theft from someone else. The partner is an object of pleasure. Such experiences are usually unsatisfactory, furtive, painful, incomplete, partial, frustrating, destructive (especially for the girl), and destroy the potential of the sex act within marriage. Walter Trobisch says, "Love does not grow out of sex, but love must grow into sex. . . . Love can be hurt by sex. It can be killed by sex. Therefore, love has to be protected."[2] Why wait for sex? Wait to be free—free from guilt and frustration—free to give totally of yourself.

Purpose of Sex

The expression of love during courtship calls for self-control, self-discipline, and respect. Love needs protection. Sex is part of God's plan and sex is good. It is deeper than just physical because it is so total it must be

[2]From *Love Is a Feeling to Be Learned* by Walter Trobisch, © Editions Trobisch, Baden-Baden, Germany. Used by permission of Inter-Varsity Press, U.S.A.

fulfilled only under conditions which make a total union possible—marriage. Sex makes two people one. You can only give your total self to one person.

Petting is actually preparing the body physically, emotionally, and mentally for sexual intercourse. Heavy petting should be avoided until after marriage.

4. What purpose of sex is given in Genesis 1:27, 28?

5. Read Proverbs 5:15-19 and Song of Solomon 7:6-10 and summarize another purpose.

6. In 1 Corinthians 7:2 what command is given to married couples to keep them from temptation and adultery?

7. Matthew 19:5, 6 talks of oneness. How can the physical union contribute to fulfilling this oneness?

Facing Temptation

Read 1 Corinthians 10:13; James 4:7.

8. a. Predetermine how far I will go
   b. Understand the male sex and reactions . . . be careful in dress and actions
   c. Don't engage in heavy petting
   d. Choose my activities and company wisely
   e. Read wholesome books—deal with my thoughts (Matthew 5:28-30)
   f. Beware of masturbation—it causes guilt, fantasy, and habits. Gini Andrews discusses this in *Your Half of the Apple.*[3]

Present Condition

If you are already unchaste, read:

[3]Gini Andrews, *Your Half of the Apple* (Grand Rapids: Zondervan, 1972).

a. 2 Peter 1:9
b. Revelation 12:10—Christ died for your sins
c. 1 John 1:7-9—ask for cleansing and forgiveness and God's healing
d. Walk in the Spirit

My Application

Commit this area of your life to God. He wants to help you remain pure until your marriage. He wants the best for you—to protect you. Wait for his timing. Ask God's protection when you are on a date, and for his strength to do what is right. Ask the Holy Spirit to control you daily. Ephesians 5:18; Galatians 5:16

Her Preparation for Marriage
LESSON 11: Are You Ready to Say I Do?

Marriage can be a "little bit of Heaven on earth." God designed marriage so that the man and woman would complement each other—two unique individuals can blend into one unit. That is why opposite temperaments often attract each other. This can give you a beautiful balance in marriage—or be the cause of many problems! Divorce is prevalent today; as Christians we need to know how to succeed in our marriages.

Marriage

Let's look at forces that have influenced your viewpoint of marriage.

1. Fill out the chart concerning my parents' marriage and relationship.

PARENTS' MARRIAGE

Strengths	Weaknesses

2. Think of one ideal marriage I know, and describe.
3. List 5 things I want in my own marriage.

a.

b.

c.

d.

e.

4. What should I look for in a husband? Summarize briefly the characteristics.

a. 2 Corinthians 6:14, 15; Deuteronomy 7:3, 4

b. 1 Corinthians 9:25; Galatians 5:23

c. Psalm 119:9

d. Romans 12:1, 2

e. Proverbs 21:25

f. 1 Timothy 3:3

g. Titus 2:7, 8

h. 1 Timothy 4:12-14

Any others you can think of?

Roles

The prime role of the man is loving, intelligent leadership. He has the responsibility of provision, and chooses the values and emphasis of the home. The man is ultimately responsible to God for the condition of his home. He is responsible to obey the command of God to love his wife; if he does this, he will be sensitive to the needs of his wife, and responsive to her as she shares these needs with him.

The woman needs the security of her husband's love. Her duty is to be submissive—so her man can be a man. She needs to feed her husband all the information and facts she can so he can make intelligent decisions. She must honestly communicate her needs to her husband, and not conceal and suppress them, allowing them to fester into bitterness and anger.

44

God's Chain of Command

5. In 1 Corinthians 11:3 and Ephesians 5:21-33, list in biblical order God's chain of command.

6. In 1 Corinthians 11:3 and Ephesians 5:23, 24, what two examples of submission are given?

In Larry Christensen's book on the family, he says the essential reasons for the wife's submission are for her protection: 1. Physical protection (from attack or danger); 2. Emotional protection (from attacks of the community or neighbors as well as from her own children); 3. Spiritual protection (1 Corinthians 11:10, referring to her covering—submission—which protects her from the evil angels). When she is under his headship she can move in the spiritual realm and her ministry with authority and freedom. She is protected to a great extent from Satan's attack.[1]

Responsibilities of a Wife

In order to meet the needs of her husband, the wife must realize what these needs are. A man has several basic needs, the greatest being his need for *admiration.* He desires admiration for his physical body, his achievements, his abilities, his spiritual qualities, and his personality. If his wife does not supply his need for admiration, he will get it elsewhere, legitimately or otherwise.

Another need he has is for *acceptance,* total and complete acceptance of himself as a person. Full acceptance sets a man free and gives him the confidence he needs in his work.

[1]Reprinted by permission from *The Christian Family* by Larry Christensen, © 1970, Bethany Fellowship, Inc., Minneapolis, Minnesota 55438.

Several good books discuss the husband's needs and how to meet them, such as *The Total Woman*[2], and *To Have and to Hold*.[3] He will thrive and blossom if these needs are being met.

Problems in Marriage

The root cause of most problems in marriage is self-centeredness. Tim LaHaye discusses this in *How to Be Happy Though Married*.[4]

Communication

In a happy marriage there is good communication. Good books on communication are *Cherishable Love and Marriage*[5] and *The Art of Understanding Your Mate*.[6]

7. Look up these verses and summarize attitudes and principles regarding communication.
   a. Ephesians 4:26-32
   b. Proverbs 10:19
   c. Proverbs 15:1, 4
   d. Proverbs 14:29
   e. Proverbs 19:13; 21:9

During your courtship the art of communication should be developed.

Finances

If the priorities are right there will be fewer problems.

[2]Marabel Morgan, *The Total Woman,* (New Jersey: Revell, 1973), ch. 4-7.

[3]Jill Renich, *To Have and to Hold* (Grand Rapids: Zondervan, 1972), ch. 2, 3.

[4]Tim LaHaye, *How to Be Happy Though Married* (Tyndale; Wheaton, 1968).

[5]David Augsburger, *Cherishable Love and Marriage* (Scottdale, Pa: Herald Press, 1971).

[6]Cecil Osborne, *The Art of Understanding Your Mate* (Grand Rapids: Zondervan, 1970).

8. What is my source of wealth? Ecclesiastes 5:19; Deuteronomy 8:17, 18.

9. What should be my attitude towards money? 1 Timothy 6:6-10.

10. Hebrews 13:5 tells me what my priorities should be. List.

Sexual Relationship

The sex life is like a barometer showing the health of the total relationship. To prevent problems, you each need to be aware of your partner's needs and the differences of each one's response. You need to be aware of the basics of conception, contraceptives, and sexual intercourse, but most important of all is simply a desire to give of yourself to your mate and make him happy. Sex is basically a mental attitude. Excellent books on these areas are *Everything You Need to Know to Stay Married and Like It,*[7] *Sexual Happiness in Marriage,*[8] and *The Essence of Marriage.*[9]

Application

1. What attitudes towards marriage do I need to change?

2. Do I need to change my standards in choosing a mate?

3. How can I now begin preparing for a happy marriage relationship?

[7]Wiese & Steinmetz, *Everything You Need to Know to Stay Married and Like It* (Grand Rapids: Zondervan, 1972).
[8]Herbert Miles, *Sexual Happiness in Marriage* (Grand Rapids: Zondervan, 1967).
[9]J. A. Fritze, *The Essence of Marriage* (Grand Rapids: Zondervan, 1969).

The Woman Fulfilled in Marriage

Her Attitudes
LESSON 12: Complete, Don't Compete!

As we accept ourselves as women, we find we do not need to compete with our husband, and we also realize we are not inferior but equals—who have different roles. The wife has the privilege of complementing and completing her husband. Our attitudes towards our husband will make the difference between a fulfilling and happy relationship with our husband or a frustrating, unhappy marriage.

Acceptance

Full acceptance sets a man totally free to be himself and gives him the confidence he needs in his work. Nagging is the opposite of acceptance.

1. List all the qualities I like about my husband.
2. Now, as I hand God my husband's faults and forget them (by an act of my will), I will determine not to try to change him.

Read 1 Corinthians 13:4-8 and discuss.

Admiration

Admiration is a man's greatest need!

3. List some manly traits I am proud of in my husband (physical, achievements, abilities, successes, spiritual qualities):

4. What was the last thing I praised my husband for?

5. From Genesis 2:18, think of ways a woman can complement and complete her husband.

Read Ephesians 5:33, Amplified. Also Philippians 4:4, 6-8.

Home Atmosphere

The home should be a safe place—a refuge.

6. What is the influence of the woman in the home?
   a. Atmosphere: Proverbs 24:3, 4; 15:4; 16:24
   b. Spiritually: 1 Peter 3:1; 8-10
   c. Emotionally: Proverbs 12:4; Titus 2:4; 1 Timothy 6:6-8

7. What do these verses say about living with a contentious woman?
   a. Proverbs 21:19, 9
   b. Proverbs 25:24
   c. Proverbs 27:15
   d. Proverbs 19:13

8. Define contentious.

9. What are some causes of contention in the home?

10. What was the most recent "contentious" thing I did to my husband and why?

My Application

1. Are there any attitudes I desire to change?

2. List four specific things I can do to promote a positive atmosphere.

Additional material on attitudes can be found in: Darien B. Cooper, *You Can Be the Wife of a Happy Husband* (Wheaton: SP Publications, Inc., 1974).

Jill Renich, *To Have and to Hold* (Grand Rapids: Zondervan, 1972).

Her Submission
LESSON 13: Did You Promise to Obey?

Male and female are equal in status and spiritual grace but different in creation and function. Submission is part of God's plan for a happy marriage.

God's Chain of Command
1. In 1 Corinthians 11:3 and Ephesians 5:21-33, list in biblical order God's chain of command.
2. In Genesis 3:16 what authority pattern is established? Who was to rule?

Submission
God gives women the choice of being submissive to their husbands or of being independent—Christ himself chose to be submissive. Even as the wife is to be submissive, the husband is to have a sacrificial love towards his wife. Also, he is held responsible for the wife and children. The woman's submission to her husband is unto the Lord himself. Through her submission she shows her trust in the Lord, and remains under his protection. (See Bob Mumford's book, *Living Happily Ever After,* pp. 23-30.)[1]

[1]Bob Mumford, *Living Happily Ever After* (Old Tappan, New Jersey: Fleming H. Revell Co., 1973), pp. 23-30.

3. In 1 Corinthians 11:3 and Ephesians 5:23, 24, what two examples of submission are given? Did either of these examples feel it is "demeaning" to be submissive?

4. Define submission.

5. Is submission an attitude or an act?

6. What command is given to wives in Ephesians 5:21-33, and Colossians 3:18, 19?

7. How is it to be done? Ephesians 5:22

8. List three or four specific situations where it is difficult for me to be submissive to my husband.

9. What should I do if I know my husband is making a wrong decision?

10. How far do I go in being submissive to a non-Christian husband? (Shirley Rice has a good chapter in her book on this area.)[2]

11. List some specific ways a wife can help her husband assume his role as head of the home.

Problems in Submission

12. How is my will involved in submission? Can I change? see:
   a. Romans 6:12-14
   b. Galatians 2:20
   c. Philippians 2:13
   d. Romans 12:1, 2

13. Paraphrase Ephesians 5:33, using as many synonyms for reverence or respect as I can. (Amplified Version is good.)

[2]Shirley Rice, *The Christian Home,* (Norfolk Christian Schools, Virginia, 1965), pp. 35-37.

14. How does God feel when I don't forgive my husband and carry bitterness and resentment in my heart? Matthew 6:14, 15; Mark 11:24, 25

TO WORK OR NOT TO WORK is a question many women face, and it is very important that if they do choose to work, their husbands are in favor of it, and also that the women's homes, husbands, and children still receive first priority.

Communication

Although the Christian woman should be submissive to her husband, she should share in the "fact-finding" necessary as a basis for good decisions. Communication is important—it develops our love and understanding for our mate, and also helps us have oneness of purpose and goals.

Finances

Many a husband is pressured into long hours or holding down two jobs in order to satisfy his wife's material demands. Let's keep our priorities straight!

15. What should be my attitude towards money? 1 Timothy 6:6-10
16. Hebrews 13:5 tells me what my priorities should be. List.

My Application

1. Do I have any resentment or bitterness that needs to be cleansed and removed? Confess it, claim God's forgiveness and cleansing (1 John 1:7-9) and then ask my husband to forgive me. Then praise God!
2. In what areas do I need to change my attitudes?

Her Sex Life
LESSON 14: Bedtime Barometer

The Hebrew word for sexual intercourse means "to know"—in the depths of their being. It is the opportunity to totally give of oneself to the one you love and enter into a total and most intimate relationship. The sex life is like a barometer—showing the health of the total marriage.

Purpose of Sex

1. For procreation
   a. What was God's command in Genesis 1:27, 28?
2. For pleasure
   a. Read Proverbs 5:15-20 and summarize.
   b. Read Song of Solomon 7:6-10. List thoughts that indicate the enjoyment of the physical relationship.
3. To prevent immorality
   a. In 1 Corinthians 7:2 what command is given to keep one from temptation and adultery?

A woman who does not meet her husband's needs sexually opens the door for Satan's attack on her marriage.

4. To provide intimate fellowship.

a. See Genesis 4:1; Matthew 19:5, 6; and 1 Corinthians 7:3-5.

Sexual Purity in Marriage

God instructs us to maintain sexual purity—for our protection and happiness.

5. a. From the following verses, summarize reasons for maintaining sexual purity.
   1 Thessalonians 4:3-8
   1 Corinthians 6:9, 13, 18-20
   Galatians 5:19
   Proverbs 6:26-32
   Hebrews 13:4

Keys to a Good Sexual Relationship

1. My relationship to God
   a. a personal relationship to Jesus Christ
   b. healthy attitudes—no bitterness or resentment

2. Communication
   a. What part does it play in the sexual relationship?

3. Understanding differences
   a. Am I aware of differences in my husband's needs from my own needs? (frequency, for variety, reactions, arousal, etc.)

4. Understanding my hangups
   a. List major thoughts and concepts regarding sex that I grew up with.
   b. List fears I have or have had regarding sex.
   c. List excuses I use to avoid sexual intercourse with my husband.

Results of a Good Sexual Relationship

1. Brings comfort; security of being loved
2. Better physical health (takes away tension)
3. Oneness in marriage, builds strong foundation
4. Develops inner self-confidence, acceptance
5. Develops self-esteem, self-worth

My Assignment

1. Discuss with my husband problem areas of sex.
2. If my desire isn't up to his, ask the Lord's help.
3. Prepare mentally and physically for my love time.
4. Ask God to deliver me from my hangups and cleanse my wrong attitudes.
5. Read some of the following books:
   Everything You Need to Know to Stay Married and Like It, Wiese & Steinmetz
   Physical Unity in Marriage, Shirley Rice
   Power of Sexual Surrender, Marie Robinson
   Sex without Fear, S. A. Lewin
   Sexual Happiness in Marriage, Herbert Miles
   Total Woman, Marabel Morgan
   Sensitive Woman, Sandra Chandler
   Handbook to Marriage, Theo. Bovet
   How to Be Happy Though Married, Tim LaHaye
   The Essence of Marriage, J. A. Fritze

The Woman Fulfilled
As a Mother

Her Spiritual Responsibilities
and Blessings
LESSON 15: As the Twig Is Bent

Raising children is a great responsibility but also a privilege and joy.

1. List some ways my children have been a spiritual blessing to me.

2. In what ways can a Christian mother be a blessing to her children?

3. What are several principles of character development (attitudes and actions) that I think are important and would like to develop in my children?

   a.

   b.

   c.

   d.

4. What is the importance of developing my child's self-image? (*Hide or Seek*[1] contains much valuable information about this.)

5. Name some things that I remember from my childhood that helped me in my character development.

6. In what ways am I to train my children?

[1]James Dobson, *Hide or Seek* (Old Tappan, New Jersey: Fleming Revell Co., 1974).

   a. 2 Timothy 1:5; Proverbs 22:6
   b. Deuteronomy 6:6, 7
   c. Ephesians 6:4

Truly the greatest responsibility Christian parents have is to introduce their child to Jesus Christ as his Savior, and to nurture his development spiritually.

7. What is my responsibility as a parent in the following verses?
   a. Proverbs 31:1
   b. Deuteronomy 6:20

Children learn not so much from what we tell them, as from our example.

8. Look up the following verses and see what influence the parent had on the child.
   a. Ezekiel 16:44
   b. 1 Kings 22:52
   c. 2 Chronicles 20:32

Family Worship

"The family that prays together stays together." There are many good books, records, and tapes available today to help a family have a varied and stimulating family worship together. Each family has to adapt their time together to their own schedule and needs but it should include a meaningful prayer time and Scripture. *The Christian Family*[2] has some excellent suggestions for the family worship.

9. Describe a meaningful family worship I have experienced.

[2]Larry Christensen, *The Christian Family* (Minneapolis: Bethany Fellowship, 1970).

10. What improvements need to be made in the family worship time in my home?

My Application

1. Do my husband and I have long-range goals for our children's character development?

2. How am I praying for my children's spiritual growth?

3. What specifically did I do today to build up my child's self-image?

4. Claim a Scripture that has been meaningful to me.

Training and Discipline
LESSON 16: Spare the Rod...

Obedience begins in the home. God holds us responsible for disciplining our children—and if we don't we will reap the results. Obedience is not optional and does not depend upon our own perfection. Did you know an obedient child is a happy child? Also, a child who has learned obedience to his parents finds it much easier to be obedient to the Lord when he is older.

1. Define discipline.

2. Define training.

3. What command is given to children? Colossians 3:20; Exodus 20:12.

4. When should we discipline? Ecclesiastes 8:11.

5. Paraphrase Proverbs 22:6.

6. What do the following verses say about discipline?
   a. Proverbs 13:24
   b. Proverbs 20:11
   c. Proverbs 19:18
   d. Proverbs 29:15
   e. Proverbs 29:17

7. For what reasons should we spank?

8. Read 1 Samuel 3:12, 13. Why was Eli held responsible for the wrongdoing of his sons?

9. What is one warning in discipline? Colossians 3:21; Ephesians 6:4

10. Is it important for parents to be in agreement over discipline? Why?

11. How have I applied principles of rewards and motivation? (*Dare to Discipline*[1] has some excellent suggestions about this.)

12. How much control should be exercised regarding my children's friends, amusements, and social life?

Sex Education

13. How do my husband and I handle sex education in our home?

Assignment

1. Claim these promises as a parent:
   a. Proverbs 3:5, 6
   b. Colossians 1:27
   c. James 1:5

2. Buy some good books on sex education for my children (such as the series by Concordia,[2] *Susie's Babies*,[3] *How To Tell Your Children about Sex*,[4] Broadman Press series,[5] *From Parent to Child about Sex*,[6] and *Almost Twelve*.[7]

[1]James Dobson, *Dare to Discipline* (Wheaton: Tyndale House, 1970).
[2]Concordia Sex Education Series.
[3]E. Margaret Clarkson, *Susie's Babies* (Grand Rapids: Wm. Eerdmans Publishing, 1960).
[4]Clyde Narramore, *How To Tell Your Children About Sex* (Grand Rapids: Zondervan, 1958).
[5]Broadman Press Series, (Nashville, Tennessee: Broadman Press, 1973).
[6]Wilson Grant, *From Parent to Child about Sex*.
[7]Kenneth Taylor, *Almost Twelve* (Wheaton: Tyndale, 1968).

My Application

1. Are my husband and I in agreement over child discipline?

2. Do I discipline immediately or wait until I am angry?

3. Do I reward good behavior with praise?

Prayer List